West Country Hauntings

PETER UNDERWOOD

Bossiney Books · Launceston

Other ghostly titles from Bossiney Books

Ghost hunting South-West Michael Williams
Ghostly encounters Peter Underwood
Ghosts of Bodmin Moor Michael Williams
Ghosts of Cornwall Peter Underwood
Ghosts of Devon Peter Underwood
Ghosts of North Devon Peter Underwood
Ghosts of Somerset Peter Underwood
Psychic phenomena of the West Michael Williams
Supernatural Dartmoor Michael Williams

Author's acknowledgements

The author gratefully acknowledges the interest and help of the following friends, correspondents and Ghost Club Society members who have generously given their time and answered many questions during the compilation of this work: Mrs Beverlie Atkins, Mr M P Barnard, Miss Maria Brookwell, Reverend Dr A T P Byles, Mrs Mary Campbell, Geoffrey and Pamela Cole, Mr Paul Cowling, Reverend Peter Lafevre Eustice, Lee and Jacqueline Gosden, Venerable Richard Hawkins, Commander John R Hoover, Freda and Steuart Kiernander, Mrs Sue Knight, Mrs Jean Monk, Mrs Wendy Seels, Mrs Lucy Sellin, Mr A J Tough BA, Mr A B Venning, Mr and Mrs Thomas Walker, Mr John West, Michael and Sonia Williams.

Reprinted 2005
This edition first published 2004 by
Bossiney Books Ltd, Langore, Launceston, Cornwall PL15 8LD
www.bossineybooks.com
Original edition published 1986 by Bossiney Books
© 1986, 2004 Peter Underwood
All rights reserved
ISBN 1-899383-64-6
Cover design by Heards Design Partnership
Printed in Great Britain by R Booth Ltd, Mabe, Penryn, Cornwall TR10 9HH

Introduction

Never before has there been such admiration and concern for our natural and national splendours and never before has there been such widespread interest in the ghost lore and legend of our countryside. Nowhere is this more evident than in the glorious West Country.

I can look back to nearly 50 years ago when we spent wonderful holidays with our children in Cornwall and for years my wife and I journeyed West twice a year. It was something we looked forward to, something that brightened the long, dark days of winter, for the West Country is unchanging in some ways but different in others. The splendid coastal and inland scenery always delighted the eye and we invariably found new delights in the way of unspoilt places off the beaten track and, not infrequently, a fascinating house with a ghost or haunting legend.

Cornwall, Devon and Somerset all have a mysterious and sometimes sinister air. There is something soft and alluring about Devon, something secret and irresistible about Somerset and something wild and strange about Cornwall. The West Country has some of the most remarkable, convincing and enduring hauntings anywhere in Britain.

I could take you to houses where the atmosphere of the past is so strong that it has affected occupants for generations; I could introduce you to people who have walked and talked with ghosts not once but many times; and I could lead you to parts of the West Country where something has remained for centuries that still affects practically everyone who goes there. These are just some of the secret places waiting to be found in the highways and byways of this splendid area.

The West Country can call you back again and again and you will never be disappointed. It offers impressive and varied scenery and just about every kind of ghostly manifestation under the sun. I wish you luck as you wander round, for almost anywhere in that special area the barriers between this world and another, stranger, world seem somehow less tangible...

Peter Underwood
The Savage Club, 1 Whitehall Place, London SW1A 2HD

Banwell, Somerset

Here, where the abbey has been reputedly haunted for many years, a nearby house has a stairway that is, or was, decidedly haunted. Shaw Desmond told me of a night he spent exploring the mysterious menace of the haunted staircase and I cannot do better than quote from notes I made at the time, in the sombre surroundings of the Ghost Club Society.

'There was always about the house a silence, brooding, alive. It was a silence not of the grave, but of the living-dead. It is a phenomenon which every searcher of such haunted houses recognises.

'My hostess asked me whether I would like her to show me and some other guests "The Scented Staircase", as she called it, where she told us she had herself been hurled down the stairs by hands invisible, and she warned not only myself but others in the house never, under any circumstances, to ascend alone. When asked for an explanation, she had merely said quietly: "You see, there is Something at the head of the stairs always waiting."

'It was only later that I learned that some people, upon reaching the top of the stairs, found themselves almost resistlessly inclined to fling themselves over the top and down the immensely deep well beneath, in which a light was always kept burning day and night to break up any dangerous spirit manifestations.

'In spite of what I had been told I decided to make an attempt to ascend the staircase alone. The whole place had sunk to rest in a midnight silence that "could be cut with a knife" and I felt myself alone, not only in that house, it seemed, but in the whole world. It may have been fancy, but as I quietly made my way to the staircase, it seemed to me that I was being trailed. Of course, that was probably silly – as I told myself – yet I was not fool enough to pretend that I was not followed, for I was quite sure that I was. But by what?

'When I stopped for a moment, I could hear nothing but the breathing of the house like the breathing of a living thing. And I am prepared to say, as Fichte the philosopher once said, that such things as old houses, and even the earth itself, are living creatures with "souls"; but what sort of soul?

4

'I had given myself my word of honour that, come what might, I would not only ascend those stairs, but also I would go still farther, up through the house to the roof itself if possible.

'One thing I recall with extraordinary clarity. I found myself looking at a tiny light hanging in mid-air and showing a well seemingly running up into the darkness.

'Before me was the staircase with its beams and balustrades and I could see dimly above me something that seemed to move slowly from side to side. As soon as I was on the first step I was aware of the scent of the strange wood of which the stairway was composed; it filled my nostrils and nauseated me. It was a sweet, slightly sickly scent.

'In a moment I was overwhelmed with a desire to beat instant retreat and return to my room. But pride is a strange stimulant; it can destroy – but it can also save. The fact was that, although a coward, I was too proud to go back! I knew that if I did so I would not be able to face myself again.

'And then, as I mounted the second step, I found to my relief that nothing further frightened me; and so I ascended, step by step. I think I must have ascended a dozen steps or so when I felt something slip on to my shoulders. Yet, it was not quite like that; it was more an envelopment, as though a blanket had been thrown across them. It was imagination, wasn't it?

'I only knew that there came over me heavy fear – the real thing. Nor could I say that it felt like anything living – nothing, for instance, like a ghost. It was more an envelopment of something unknown.

'As I reached the last flight, I found myself rapidly losing not only breath, but also the resistance-power which had so far carried me on. Now I knew that I was face to face with the powers of darkness, and that if they once got the upper hand, anything might happen – even that passing through what should be "death's friendly little portal".

'There was a landing on my left; on it stood some ancient piece of furniture – long disused; before me a high smooth facade of wall; in it what seemed to my inflamed imagination to be a high narrow door leading to the roofs – those roofs I had sworn to reach – yet, a long time afterwards, upon a daylight visit, I was to find the door which was so plain to see that night had vanished; in its place a massive door leading not to the roofs, but to the interior of the building. I have never been able to explain this.

'The pressure to run down the stairs became nearly intolerable. It was like a physical pressure on my body, which had grown steadily weaker. But I felt I had to go through that door so I turned the handle… Thank God! It was locked! So pride and honour were satisfied; I could return to my room in peace. Yet this was not the end.

'As I turned to walk down the stairs I suddenly went weak. I found myself to be a coward where I thought I had been brave. It was as though I had had a hard left hook to the solar plexus. I just could no longer keep my feet. So, half falling forward, I got my arms over the broad balustrade which overhung the gulf in which the light burned. I used the balustrade as support, for I could scarcely find the top of the stairs.

'And then it came. At last I knew the menace of the scented staircase. It was the desire to fling myself down into that gulf that waited for me… I had the presence of mind instantly to let myself sink down on the floor behind the balustrade. Then I crawled to the head of the stairs and, sitting on each step, and holding on to the balusters as I went, I kept my mind from thinking of the well over the side, and, literally step by step, in ungainly and cowardly fashion, I came down the stairs flight by flight, until I reached the bottom.

'Then, whitefaced and badly shaken, I made my way back to my room. There may well be those who will laugh at me but they have never felt what I felt and known what I knew that night, and I hope never to feel that way again.'

Barnstaple, Devon

In 1984 I received a letter from a young married lady from Barnstaple. She had read my *Ghosts of Devon*, published by Bossiney Books, and as her home town was not mentioned she was kind enough to send me details of a personal experience. I cannot do better than quote from her letter:

'My father has a small contract cleaning business and in the evenings I help him to clean the offices of a small business in the town. About twelve months ago [June 1983] as we entered the offices as usual one evening, I said to Dad, without really knowing why I did so, "It feels as though someone has hanged themselves in here…"

'Later, while in the kitchen area, I distinctly felt someone standing behind me and I knew without turning round that it was a man; I felt him put out a hand to touch me to attract my attention so I quickly said, "It's okay, I know you're there," whereupon my mysterious visitor withdrew his hand and I continued to speak to him. I asked him what his name was and I received the name Eric White. He intimated that he had been a bank clerk and, unbeknown to me at the time, the business premises we were in had once been an old bank in the 1800s. Eric had committed suicide by hanging himself there in 1878, he told me, when he was accused of embezzlement. He wasn't guilty of the crime but he and his family were so hounded that Eric eventually took his own life. He was sad because he wanted people to know that he was innocent; in fact his eldest son James had actually committed the crime but he wasn't found out until years later.

'Eric intimated that his wife's name was Margaret and they had four children named James, Eric, Ann and Elizabeth. I informed Eric that his innocence couldn't really be proved now as it was such a long time ago but I said I would find out all I could about the matter. Armed with the details that Eric had given to me about himself and his family I went along to our local library and examined local parish records. After some painstaking research with the help of one of the senior staff, we found Eric's name on an old census form for the address of the old bank – he had lived above it – and in the Births and Deaths registers I also found records of his children.

'The senior library official then added further proof, for his own father had been a bank clerk at that particular bank some fifty years after Eric's death and he had asked his mother what she knew of the old bank and if there had ever been a ghost story connected with it.

'His mother told him that she could remember his father talking about a customer who once came in asking if anyone had seen the ghost of a man who had hanged himself on the premises. Only after learning this from his mother had the library official told her of my visit and of my meeting with Eric.

'A few nights later I was cleaning the same offices with Dad as usual and as I walked down the passage to attend to the gents' toilet, I pushed open the door and saw a man's body swinging out towards me; it was the body of a man who had hanged himself and it gave me an awful fright. I turned and ran up the passage shouting, "Dad! Dad!" until I found him… When I had got my breath, I marched back down to the toilets and told Eric off in no uncertain terms. I was very angry.

'His explanation was that he wanted to show me how he had died. I said that my imagination was quite adequate on that score. On subsequent visits Eric was in the office from time to time and each evening as we went in we'd say "Hello". He seemed pleased to see us. In time, I felt sad leaving him behind when we returned home, but as time passed Eric seemed much happier because he knew we believed in his innocence. However, he still felt sad that he was separated from his family, so I said we'd see what we could do.

'I made enquiries and sought to discover whether Eric could find peace and proceed to the Other Side and be with his family. Soon we noticed that Eric was no longer around at the business premises; at first I missed him, but I was pleased to think that he was at last with his family.

'It was some months later when Eric came for a final visit. Dad and I went into the office on the evening of 11 December, my birthday. I was walking just ahead of Dad to attend to the light switches which are situated at the far end of the main office. As I put my hand out to put the lights on I bumped into the form of a man; he seemed just as solid as you or I but in those few seconds it registered with me that this was Eric and with him were his wife and family. He was so happy that it simply radiated from him. All the forms were seen by me to be in the clothes that they would have worn in their own time. It was a very happy experience and Eric said, "For your celebration, Sue." It was my birthday and it was a lovely gesture which I shall never forget.

'So Eric has gone for good and while it sometimes seems very quiet without him pottering around, I'm just glad that I was able to help him.'

Bishops Lydeard, near Taunton, Somerset

The West Country is rich in stories of spectral dogs: the Devon Folklore Register alone lists reported sightings at Bradford, Bradworthy, Bridestowe, Cockington, Dartmoor, Lewtrenchard, Lydford, Newton St Cyres, Okehampton, Sheepstor, Stowford, Tavistock, Torrington, Uplyme, Washfield and Widecombe-in-the-Moor! However, it is unlikely, I am told by her daughter, Mrs Beverlie Atkins, that her mother – who died twenty-five years ago – would have heard of such phantoms when she had her never-to-be-forgotten experience.

Mrs Rosina Wyndham Bolton resided at the Old Forge with her husband who was attached to the Foreign Office before his retirement, and it was at the Old Forge that Mrs Bolton saw a ghost dog, after they had been living at Bishops Lydeard for some six years. Mrs Bolton was in business for most of her life, conducting a model school in London, later acting as public relations officer for a well-known corsetry firm, and still later running a correspondence course in customer psychology for their sales people.

'I should hate to think I might have extra-sensory perception,' Mrs Bolton admitted in 1969, 'but the fact is that both my husband and I heard this dog on several occasions, padding along the upstairs corridor, but I am the only one who has seen it. It doesn't bother us at all. We were told when we moved in that the place was haunted by a little old woman – there was no mention of a phantom dog! The property is very old and historic; it used to be part of an old priory that stood on the site of the church. Some twenty years ago a cavalier's thigh boot with a silver spur was found in one of the walls by the previous owners when they were making structural alterations.

'The first time I saw the dog I was standing in the kitchen about 6.30 one morning in April. I was getting ready to catch the early train for a business trip to Edinburgh when I happened to glance out of the window and was surprised to see a dog go loping across the lawn with its nose to the ground! It was a very large dog, bigger than an Alsatian and a sort of grey colour. As the garden is completely walled and the gates were locked, I wondered whose dog it was and how on earth it had got in.

'Then I noticed that our own dog, Sam, who hates intruders, was sitting shivering in his basket with his hair on end, watching it too. I didn't have time to think any more about it until I was on the train. Then my curiosity was aroused. I went into the museum at Edinburgh, and looked through all the dog pictures they had. I knew I had seen that sort of dog before but could not think where. I found it in an old print – an exact likeness – and it was described as a German boar hound, very popular as a hunting dog in the sixteenth and seventeenth centuries, now almost extinct.'

A few weeks later, in exactly the same circumstances, Mrs Bolton saw the same dog. 'Again I had an early train to catch and looking out of the window on a sunny, slightly misty spring morning, I saw the animal again – but this time I was prepared. I ran quickly to the window to see where it went and as it reached the far wall – suddenly there was no dog there! Not a sign of it. I dashed out into the garden. No sign anywhere and both the gates were closed. Sam, who is always glad of an excuse to run out of doors, just sat in his basket, shivering. This time I had had a really good look at the dog and it was rather like an Irish wolfhound but thicker set and with a slightly more blunted nose. But the thing that really shook me was that I distinctly remember seeing the far wall through the dog as it ran across the lawn, again with its nose to the ground.'

Mr Bolton said at the time that he had 'heard a dog walking on the polished boards of the landing when Sam was locked in the kitchen' but he could throw no light on the dog his wife had seen. From what his wife had told him and the reaction of their own dog, Mr Bolton felt there was something about the incident that was quite inexplicable.

Mrs Atkins, writing to me in 1986, said that Sam was a Border Collie, highly intelligent and he would normally fight any dog on sight – but not, it seems, a dog that was not of this world.

Blisland, near Bodmin

'Into Bodmin,' the old folks used to say, 'and out of this world.' Most certainly the old capital of Cornwall still has a sleepy, smouldering and unreal atmosphere with its massive former prison that could tell some strange tales if only the stones could talk; and there have been stories of psychic disturbances within those old walls as well as disturbances of a more worldly kind.

A property at Blisland that used to be called the Tom Rose Farm was once part of Glynn Barton Farm, owned by the Linne family, or so I am told by a correspondent who lived on the farm. Mr and Mrs Thomas Walker left Glynn Barton Farm in the 1950s and moved to North Devon; they didn't keep in touch with the Linne family apart from a yearly Christmas card, but when they were on holiday in Cornwall in 1971 they paid a surprise visit to their former employers, meeting the son Robin and daughter Elizabeth again after a long time. They spent a pleasant couple of hours talking about former days and the strange stories that used to circulate at Blisland about the Tom Rose, or 'Tumrose', Farm.

It seems that a man named Tom Rose used to own the property and, as he grew old, his young relatives wanted him to leave but he always refused to go, saying he would never leave the place. It seems that something of his presence remained at the house long after the death of his physical body.

Mrs Walker can remember staying there in her youth when a new wing was being built and there always seemed to be great difficulty in keeping a candle alight on the stairs; time after time something caused candles to go out whenever anyone climbed the stairs carrying one; some freak of a draught you may say, but it happened on numerous occasions for no apparent reason, and only after experiencing this phenomenon was Mrs Walker told about the the family ghost, 'Bertie'.

The two children of the resident family were never afraid of the ghost and when they heard knockings and other sounds that were attributed to it, and they were tired, they would call out, 'Shut up Bertie, we want to go to sleep,' and invariably the noises would cease.

The occupant at this time used to work at the quarry at St Breward and before he went out in the mornings he would take his wife, and Mrs Walker when she was there, a cup of tea. One particular morning she heard what she thought were his footsteps on the stairs and a loud rap sounded on the bedroom door. When Mrs Walker responded to the knocks with a call to 'Come in', the door opened, but no visible person entered the room.

Later Mrs Walker was awakened by another knock and this time it was her friend with a cup of tea. He had not come upstairs previously so Mrs Walker put down the earlier footsteps and the knock to a visit from 'Bertie' who, of course, she had not seen. In fact, I am told, the Walkers don't think anyone except dogs ever actually saw 'Bertie'.

Once Mrs Gordon, Mrs Linne's sister, took her spaniel dog with her when she visited Tom Rose Farm, but the dog could not be persuaded to enter the old part of the house. In that area his hair stood on end and he growled at something he could certainly see but which was invisible to his human companions. Nothing would make him go further than the door to the old part of the house.

On another visit to their friends at Tom Rose Farm, Mrs Walker was awakened in the middle of the night by her husband; his hair was standing almost on end and he was very white and frightened.

He gasped, 'Maria, quick, put on the light – there's someone in the room,' but of course the light revealed nothing but an empty room. Mr Walker had been awakened by the sound of footsteps climbing the stairs. He had then heard the door open and the footsteps enter; they crossed the room and approached the bed and at that moment he had awakened his wife. Next morning he would not stay in the house any longer and the Walkers packed their things and returned home. Mrs Walker tells me she tried to explain to her husband that 'Bertie' was always friendly, but he had had quite enough of ghostly antics.

Oddly enough, nothing appears to have been written about the history of the Tom Rose Farm. Shall we ever know any more about 'Bertie' and the house he haunted, I wonder?

Branscombe, near Seaton, Devon

Bovey House, an historic Elizabethan manor, originally belonged to the Abbey of Sherborne and at the back of the house there is still a raised Monks' Walk which has a peace and serenity all its own. Taken over by the Crown in 1539, following the dissolution of the monasteries, this mellow old house once belonged to Catherine Parr; it had been presented to her by King Henry VIII in 1542 as part of her dowry. Until fairly recently it was a hotel.

The Charles Room, with its magnificent coffered ceiling, is reputed to have been occupied by King Charles II. In the centre of this unique ceiling there is a large oak tree in relief and through the branches a man's face can clearly be discerned, surrounded by small figures depicting Cromwellian troops; the whole representing Boscobel Wood where Prince Charles, later King Charles II, hid in an oak tree during his flight to France after his defeat at the Battle of Worcester. During the course of his escape through Staffordshire, Worcestershire, Warwickshire and Somerset to Charmouth in Dorset, he was reputedly sheltered at Bovey House. In this room, in the 1980s, a visitor thought, just for a second, that she glimpsed the shape of a cavalier standing with a hand on the door knob; she thought it must have been her imagination although it did frighten her and a cavalier could well have been here, seeking too late the fleeing Charles.

Another legendary story, handed down here for centuries, tells of a lady resident who always dressed in black and was heavily veiled. She was accompanied by a priest and she then went away. Could she have been the tragic Henrietta Maria, queen of England and wife of Charles I? She never recovered from his death and retired to France (she was the daughter of Henri IV of France) where she died in 1669.

Bovey House has many lovely rooms, among them an apartment, tastefully furnished in blue, which is reputedly haunted by a tall but headless lady dressed in blue. She was seen by Duncan Pierce whose sister Frances recorded the event in her diary. A copy of the appropriate part of her journal is preserved at Bovey House. Frances Pierce seems to have written her diary around 1870.

Later the same figure was seen by one of the family servants who was so terrified that he nearly broke his neck in his hurry to get downstairs! And a later owner, a no-nonsense army captain, saw the ghost and promptly packed his belongings and left.

The same room in which the mysterious Blue Lady appears has occasionally become inexplicably impregnated with the scent of lavender and this perfume-like smell has been reported by several people in recent years. When I was at Bovey House in 1986 I thought the 'haunted room' had a distinct atmosphere, a stillness not apparent elsewhere in this interesting and quiet house; it was something I noticed when I entered the room for the first time and subsequently, at various times throughout several days and nights, I always had the same feeling, almost as though someone was about to appear or as though someone invisible was already there. And once, at 4.30 am as I entered the room, I noticed a faint but distinct odour of lavender. I called my wife and she noticed it too.

There is, as George Pulman says in his monumental *The Book of the Axe* (1875), 'something unusually striking in this ancient mansion grey with years'. *The Book of the Axe*, incidentally, contains a century-old print of Bovey House. In her diary Frances Pierce explains that it was a bright and sunny morning when her brother Duncan stopped suddenly on his way down to breakfast; and wondering what had happened Frances and her sister found him wearing 'a most puzzled expression'. He then explained that on passing the door of the bedroom, which happened to be open, 'his eye was caught by a wonderful gleam of blue' and he saw 'standing before the mirror of the dressing table, which was immediately opposite the door, a figure which, because of the height, he thought at first was the tallest of his sisters. "I wondered where you got that nice blue brocade," he explained. "But you didn't seem to have any head that I could see and no sooner did I stop than you quickly moved round to the other side of the room and as I followed, quite disappeared. What the dickens was it?"'

Duncan, his sister adds, was 'the most practical creature' she ever knew. 'He was absolutely healthy and cheerful and he used to say that he never had a dream in his life, waking or sleeping.'

Later the Pierces' groom, who slept in the house, 'came tearing down from the top storey, where the servants' rooms were, with his face a deathly white and fell almost fainting on to a chair. As soon as he could speak, he cried out that he had seen the ghost. At first, like Duncan, he "had thought it was Miss Frances" because of the height and she rustled past in the dim light, wearing a rich silk gown. Then he saw the figure had no head...'

'Dear old Bovey Manor' writes Frances Pierce, 'What joys it held... the wide low building of grey stone, dark ivy clinging round the stone mullioned windows whose leaded panes blinked in the wintry sun-shine...' Bovey is a lovely place and it possesses many intriguing aspects: a recess or chamber ten feet square, thirty feet down the deep well and a similar hiding place or priest's hole in one of the chimneys; an old treadmill type of well wheel in perfect condition; a water tank dated 1674; a fine rain-water head at the front of the house bearing the date the house was completed, 1592; an intimate and charming linen-fold panelled dining-room; a spacious drawing room, original-ly the medieval hall with its fine panelling and beautifully decorated Adam ceilings – all this apart from the ghosts!

Bristol

There is a fine house in one of the best residential parts of Bristol that has been reputed to be haunted for many, many years by a 'horrible, pale-faced' servant girl. She is thought to have been the natural daughter of a wealthy man who owned the house more than a hun-dred years ago. By all accounts she was a half-witted, hunch-backed creature who always seemed to wear a cheap pink dress. She lived a miserable life, half-starved and often beaten, until in the end she drowned herself in a pool in the garden or, to be more accurate, she was found drowned in a pool in the garden.

In the early part of the twentieth century a widowed colonel's wife and her three daughters took a long lease of the house and, having set-tled comfortably into the seemingly delightful property, they were more than a little surprised when they found it difficult to obtain a housemaid. During this period, soon after they had moved in, one of the daughters passed a young girl on the stairs, in a pink dress, busily sweeping away with brush and pan as though her life depended upon it. Thinking that her mother must have succeeded in obtaining a tem-porary maid, the daughter gave the girl no more than a glance, but the impression that she obtained was distinctly unfavourable. The girl appeared to be none too clean and nor was her dress; in fact she appeared distinctly untidy and sluttish, her cap was soiled and askew, she was practically hump-backed and she had a very white and unhealthy-looking face. Needless to say no temporary housemaid had actually been hired. A week or so later the ghost girl was seen by another daughter of the colonel's widow.

This time she seemed to be aware of the daughter's presence and slithered down the stairs, away from her, grinning hideously over her shoulder as she disappeared into a room and closed the door behind her. Montague Summers, that remarkable student of ghosts and haunted houses – not to mention vampires and witchcraft – told me that when he visited the house, he also saw a most repulsive-looking and dishevelled little maid in a dirty pink frock, near the front door. The creature grinned and then slipped away through a red baize door at the end of the hall.

Three weeks after the colonel's widow and her daughters moved in, one of them was alone in the house one afternoon. She went down to the basement to fetch some hot water and was astonished when she pushed open the kitchen door to see the girl in the pink dress, apparently busy cleaning the kitchen range, with her back towards the door. 'What are you doing here?' the daughter asked. The figure swung round, an impudent leer on her white face, and without a word of explanation scuttled off into an adjoining room, from which there was no other exit.

At last, the widow's daughter thought, she would catch her face to face; but the scullery was empty and there was no sign of the mysterious girl in the pink dress. Suddenly frightened, the daughter turned and ran out of the basement and upstairs to her room, pausing only to recover her breath on the landing when, to her horror, she saw, grinning at her through the landing window, thirty feet from the ground, the white face of the ghostly housemaid she had left a moment before in the kitchen!

'How I got out of the house I shall never know,' the girl told Montague Summers; she was found on the porch in a dead faint and she was so ill afterwards that she went to Brighton to recover – which took several months.

By then her mother and sisters had left the house and found another, this time without a ghost. Montague Summers told me that the family who moved in after the colonel's widow stayed less than a month; and the next tenants left abruptly within an even shorter time.

As stories of the sinister ghost spread throughout Bristol and elsewhere the house itself stood empty or, as Summers was fond of saying, empty that is except for the ghost-maid.

Chilton Polden, near Bridgwater, Somerset

Much of the county of Somerset can be seen from the top of the tower that is itself a landmark here, standing by the road the Romans made along the Polden Hills; it is a view that embraces Wells and Glastonbury, the Bristol Channel, the Welsh coast, the Mendips and the tall towers of Sedgemoor.

William Stradling collected together a wonderful hotch-potch of a museum here – sadly scattered after his death – in a curious building and he used to say that he could see one cathedral and 35 churches from the top. He would also have seen the old building long known as The Rumbling Tum Restaurant, and later as the Knight's Helm, that has stood here for some 300 years.

In 1971 Mrs Ivy Wilson and her nephew Mr Mancey ran the restaurant. They both claimed to have seen the figure of a lady in a long white dress in different parts of the building, on different occasions and under different circumstances. Often she would suddenly appear when some mundane task was being performed, such as a fireplace being cleaned out first thing in the morning. At other times she was seen in the kitchen where one witness said he felt something touch him and when he turned, there she was, standing looking, or so it seemed, at what was going on.

Another ghost here is, or was, the figure of a little old man who appeared to be incapacitated with arthritis. At the height of the disturbances physical objects were interfered with, lights in particular being inexplicably switched on and off, and once a coach party, quietly having tea, were startled when a brass plate jumped off the wall and hurtled across the room. Once, too, a friend who was staying at the restaurant woke up in the middle of the night with the distinct impression that someone or something was blowing on her face – not the most pleasant way of waking up at any time…

A later owner of the restaurant carried out renovations, and his wife, who is very sensitive to these things, felt that there was no longer a ghost there – perhaps because found behind the baker's oven during the renovations was a box containing a skeleton! This is now in a museum and that is possibly the reason why the ghost has been laid.

Croyde, Devon

In August 1985, I received a letter out of the blue from someone who had just spent a holiday at Croyde Bay. They wrote to tell me about some of the strange happenings the whole family had experienced.

Doors in the bungalow they had rented opened by themselves, no matter how securely and carefully they were closed, and once a door opened slowly by itself as three of the holidaymakers sat and watched. They said it opened very quietly and gently, sufficiently wide for a person of average bulk to enter, but no visible person was seen and certainly no human person was near the door at the time. It stood open and then after about five minutes, it was carefully and firmly closed; within seconds it gently and slowly opened again by itself. The mechanics of the door were most carefully examined and everything appeared to be in perfect order.

Two other mysterious happenings disturbed the family's holiday. One was unexplained footsteps that were repeatedly heard, heavy and distinct, making their way across the back room. The first evening, when the whole family heard these sounds for the first time, they were terrified and thought someone had broken in. When the sounds ceased they cautiously investigated but the bungalow was completely empty, apart from themselves, and nothing was out of place and nothing was missing.

During the following days and nights these sounds were heard again, on many occasions, but nothing was ever found to account for them. Once, they were heard when one of the family was in the kitchen and he quietly made his way towards the room and listened to the sounds, seemingly just on the other side of the closed door.

Quietly he opened the door but as soon as it was open an inch the sounds ceased and the room was found to be completely deserted. Other strange happenings were even more frightening. Twice, as the family were returning to the bungalow in the early evening, they all saw someone moving about inside. On the first occasion their immediate thought was that for some reason the owner had let himself in, but when they were inside the bungalow they received no reply to their calls; they found the place deserted and, as with the footsteps, nothing had been moved and nothing was missing.

The second time they saw someone moving about within the bungalow they remained outside for several minutes noting the indistinct form which seemed to be that of a man, moving across the room and then back again. Back and forth he went; each time the watchers thought that the next time they would be able to distinguish some details of the form but it moved in a halting yet swift way and they could not make out any details. Then, while one of them went to the door and let himself in, the rest watched the moving form. As soon as the door was opened, it disappeared and, as always, nothing could be found to account for it and nothing had been touched.

These visitors told me that they were rarely able to get to sleep until about three o'clock in the morning although they could not say exactly why. It was something about the atmosphere of the place that was so strange; a waiting, expectant atmosphere which kept them awake thinking that something – they knew not what – would happen at any moment. By about three o'clock in the morning the atmosphere became pleasanter and much calmer and they would all drift off to sleep… until the next night.

In December 1985 I received a letter from Mr M P Barnard of Chesham in Buckinghamshire and he was kind enough to tell me about some 'most strange happenings' that he and his family had experienced at a bungalow at Croyde. Subsequently I established that it was the same bungalow, but I will let Mr Barnard tell the story in his own words.

'Whilst on holiday in Devon this year my wife and I had some most strange happenings. We had rented a nice bungalow in Croyde, the bungalow is on the junction of two roads. After we had settled down and got the first day over, we went to bed but felt quite uneasy. Eventually we fell asleep only to waken at 3.00 am. In the nights that followed it was rare if we could sleep before this time.

'Then one evening we were sitting watching the television and could hear footsteps in the back room; they made their way across the hall and into the kitchen. The doors opened and closed by themselves. Our first thought was that it was our daughter, so we investigated, only to find Rachel fast asleep in bed.

'On another night there was such an atmosphere in the bedroom that my wife could not sleep and my daughter wouldn't even enter the room. I went in and challenged the "spirit" but couldn't get much response; this oppressive atmosphere only left the room in the early hours.

'I am only writing this letter to you because I know the bungalow has a definite ghostly resident.' In a later letter Mr Barnard emphasises that 'all the footsteps and opening and closing of doors have been witnessed by four adults including two sceptics', who were Mr Barnard's mother and father-in-law.

I am withholding the exact whereabouts of the haunted bungalow in case of other experiences from unwary visitors to Croyde.

Exmouth, Devon

According to Sabine Baring-Gould's *Devonshire Characters and Strange Events* (1908) and *Devon and Cornwall Notes and Queries* (1956-8) there is a house in Bicton Street that is said to have been haunted for over a hundred years.

The curious genesis of the haunting is generally regarded as having been the appearance of what seems to have been a headless child. This frightening apparition is said to have been seen by the cook of the family resident at Belmont House at the time, a family named Fontelautus. The cook maintained to her dying day that she was sitting quietly in the kitchen one morning in May, 1826, when the silent form entered through the open door and disappeared into the pantry.

Less than a month later, on 1 June, little Dennis Fontelautus, the younger son of the family, died before reaching the age of two. An autopsy was performed, during the course of which it was necessary to decapitate the body, and the conclusion was that little Dennis had died of water on the brain following a fall.

The little body lay in its coffin in the attic for three days before the funeral and during those days and nights the pleading voice of the dead boy was heard by the child's nursemaid, his mother and his sister Maria, apparently emanating from the attic. After the funeral the voice was still heard and Maria also saw her brother's small hand stretching out, pleadingly, from the window of the attic when she was outside the house.

In spite of the decapitation taking place during the autopsy, the family, worried by what they had seen and heard, became convinced the boy was still alive. After the body had been buried, it was subsequently exhumed and re-buried in the garden. Mr Fontelautus, a vicar, according to Sabine Baring-Gould, writing on the case in 1908, maintained that the events were due to 'demoniacal activity'. Be that as it may the house is said to have been haunted for many, many years afterwards.

In 1986, I spent several hours making enquiries and looking for Belmont House, Bicton Street, but it has either been re-named or the information I have is incorrect.

Farway, near Honiton, Devon

A 300-year-old farmhouse here, now a residential home for the elderly, is or was haunted by the ghost of two little girls who died more than a hundred years ago.

Twenty years ago the occupants were Mr and Mrs William Rugless, and Mrs Edna Rugless said at the time 'There's nothing creepy or frightening about our ghosts. We're very fond of children, having four of our own. They are more than welcome here. The noise they make doesn't usually bother me, but one afternoon I heard them run out of the bedroom and start jumping around on the landing. I went into the hall and shouted up at them to stop – and they did! Of course in their day, children were taught to be obedient.'

Edna and her husband Bill realised there was something unusual about the house almost as soon as they moved in. They both heard the distinct sound of 'scampering footsteps' in one of the bedrooms, and these sounds were usually heard just after seven in the evening, a time when small children might normally be playing before going to bed. At the same time there was often a rhythmic, creaking noise that sounded like a rocking horse being ridden. Mr and Mrs Rugless noticed that neither of their pets, a sheepdog and a cat, would go near the 'haunted' room.

A friend who was interested in psychic happenings, Mrs Mary Leman from Sutton in Surrey, came to stay and the occupants made a point of not mentioning the noises. After a few days they asked her whether she could feel anything unusual in the atmosphere of the house. Their visitor then said she had the strong impression that the ghosts of two girls, aged about four or five, were active in the house and that their names began with an E or an A.

She thought it might be interesting to ask the local vicar to check the church records to see whether he could throw any light on the matter. She had a feeling the girls were friends rather than sisters; one was wearing good quality clothes while the other's clothes were not so good. There did seem to be a very happy atmosphere in the house in spite of the ghosts. The Reverend Frederick Gilbert, it was reported, discovered from his records that two four-year-old girls belonging to the same family had died in the house; one named Elizabeth was born in 1844 and the other, Ann, in 1902. Mr Gilbert, after he had retired from the ministry, stated that he believed: 'Spirits exist in a way one cannot explain and there was certainly something quite extraordinary at the house at Farway. It is quite possible that those children were so happy in the house that they were reluctant to leave. The 58 year gap between the births makes it seem odd that they should be playmates, but we have our own limited concept of time and it may mean nothing to them.'

Should anyone enter the bedroom at a time when the noises were occurring, the sounds stopped immediately. Mr and Mrs Rugless were not at all frightened; on the contrary, they considered they were fortunate to have 'such pleasant little spirits about the place'.

Helford and Helston, Cornwall

A beautiful riverside walk leads you from Helford to Frenchman's Creek; at low tide the water may be little more than a trickle but at high tide it is a different story and the Creek can be seen as a perfect hiding place for contraband.

In days gone by the Creek is said to have been fordable at certain points, on certain tides, even where its mouth now joins the Helford River. One night, so runs the story, an old man took the short cut across the Creek. Unfortunately he had been drinking, and perhaps he had the tide wrong, but at any rate he did not return home that night.

In the morning he was found, for the tide had then receded, sitting upright in the water, with his hat still on his head, his long white beard running with water. Ever since, early on unspecified mornings, when there is an unusually low tide, the same figure has been seen where the old man met his death and also, somewhat mysteriously, his ghost has suddenly appeared in neighbouring cottages and houses that he knew during his life. He is always seen for only a few seconds and then is no longer there; some strange remnant of the past that lingers on at this idyllic spot.

There are several legends and ghost stories hereabouts concerning the redoubtable John Tregeagle and his pack of demons haunting the sands or roaming the Loe Bar, where the Pool widens as it makes its way to the sea.

The mysterious Loe Bar is also said to be haunted by a ghostly little old lady. She is reputed to have been picking wild flowers when she witnessed a terrible conflict that ended with the defeat of the evil one. In her joy the old lady ran into Helston, shouting the good news and waving her bunch of flowers.

It is in memory of that day that the people of this Cornish town have ever since danced the Flora, the Helston floral dance; and occasionally the ghostly form of a little old lady carrying a bunch of flowers has been seen running towards Helston from Loe Pool, a figure that mysteriously disappears whenever it is followed.

Kenn, Clevedon

The Drum and Monkey Inn was run for many years by an individual landlady known far and wide as 'Nellie No Change' and it is her ghost that has been reported to have been seen by residents and visitors over the years.

In 1984 both Mr and Mrs Hyde were reported to have seen the friendly phantom and from time to time their customers asked about the oddly-dressed lady whom they had glimpsed roaming through the inn, a harmless form that provoked no fear in those who saw her. She is said to have earned her nickname, 'Nellie No Change', from her habit of dealing with prosperous-looking customers, to whom she would invariably say as she took their money, 'No change!', knowing they could well afford to forego a few coppers.

As time went on she revelled in the nickname she had acquired that helped to line her pockets!

If it is indeed 'Nellie' who returns occasionally to the inn she knew for so many years it could be some fragment of her personality that still hankers for her old home or, more likely perhaps, an image of her imprinted on the atmosphere that is glimpsed under certain conditions and by certain people.

Kingsteignton, Devon

The Bell Inn here may be haunted by the screams of a young girl who, it is said, was murdered at the inn, which is believed to date from the fifteenth century.

In December 1985, when the property was being gutted for restoration, Robin Tibbs and a friend were walking past late one night when they heard a child's shrill scream; it was so spine-chilling and unexpected that they both stopped in their tracks. Mr Tibbs reportedly said at the time, 'It was really frightening. The child seemed to scream out "Mummy, Mummy, no, Mummy," and it seemed to come from the direction of The Bell Inn although the uninhabited premises were in complete darkness.'

Robin Tibbs' friend, Tom Bearne, a local butcher, thought it sounded as though a child was being ill-treated and he went immediately to investigate, 'But there was nothing there at all. It was very eerie.'

The two men feel that what they heard may be a voice from the past, perhaps something to do with the murder of a child in the vicinity. It is often the case that redecoration or alteration to a property promotes psychic phenomena; perhaps releasing in some curious way a recording of a traumatic happening that took place many years before. Interestingly enough, one of the workmen occupied on the renovation of The Bell Inn reports he had the distinct feeling that someone was watching him, especially when he was working in one particular room at the inn, although no human being was there at the time. The foreman in charge, Andrew Minchinton, said he had not personally experienced anything of a super-normal nature but he did think it 'rather odd' that all the floors but one in the building had been torn out and replaced; the one room with its original floor is the room from which the screaming is thought to have come. The flooring here was said by Andrew Minchinton to be 'too good to take up', but it has obviously since been replaced.

The inn once had the reputation of being haunted by a 'woman in white' who used to appear in one particular bedroom and there are stories of guests leaving before they had planned to do so, after they had seen, or heard, the ghost.

Lifton, Devon

Here, where new houses now stand, there occurred in 1928 a series of mysterious happenings that have never been satisfactorily explained.

The story has been recounted first-hand by Mrs Ida Roberts who vividly recalls the events taking place when she was a teenager in Lifton. One day the whole village was buzzing with the news of curious happenings at the little farmhouse then situated near the church on Duntz Hill: strange noises, objects moving of their own accord, and twigs and kidney beans appearing out of the air.

The occupant of the house, the widow of a farmer, was interviewed at the time of the occurrences and said that in the presence of herself and friends who were visiting her, twenty or more kidney beans fell, hitting some of the people present and scattering themselves all over the floor. No kidney beans were in the room at the time and no one could explain where they came from or how they got into the room.

A young girl who worked in the farmhouse, and neighbours and friends, all related how the beans came floating down from nowhere. It was suggested to the son of the house that the whole thing may have been a hoax of some sort but he replied that he was convinced it was no hoax and the family 'meant to get to the bottom of the story as it was causing mother so much worry.'

Soon news of the strange happenings spread far and wide in the West Country and Sir Arthur Conan Doyle visited the house; the vicar of a nearby church exorcised the place; a white witch from Exeter said she saw saucepans filled with vegetables put on the stove to boil – and a moment later the saucepans were mysteriously empty. The girl who worked at the house seemed to be the most affected by the disturbances – she was probably the nexus of the poltergeist – and after she left, things became less troublesome; soon the strange sounds and stranger movement of objects ceased completely, but the disturbances that caused a considerable sensation at the time were never really explained.

Littlehempston, near Totnes, Devon

The Pig and Whistle, a 400-year-old inn, has long been reputedly haunted by the ghost of a lecherous medieval monk from nearby Buckfast Abbey or rather from a former abbey or religious establishment since the present abbey is a 20th-century building.

Brother Freddie – the name he is known by – is thought to have been of French origin and to have been in the habit of using the former lodging house for his love-making; in particular he and a local farm-girl would meet at the Pig and Whistle almost daily for the duration of their affair. The monk, said to have been hunch-backed and always smiling, would slyly leave his horse nearby and enter the inn by means of a door that has since been altered into a window; a window that has been seen and heard swinging inexplicably in the breeze on a number of occasions – when there has been no breeze and on examination the window has been found tightly closed.

Brother Freddie was careful to use one particular room for his sessions of passion, a room from which, if necessary, he could escape before being caught in his amorous acts by speeding along a short tunnel to an adjoining building that served as a chapel for the holy monks of Buckfast. From this chapel, having carefully rearranged his habit, he would emerge innocently as if from prayers.

A few years ago the landlady often spoke of the 'strange atmosphere' in the place after dark and once a visitor, who happened to be psychic, said he had seen the figure of a deformed monk in the bar. For years a chair was left vacant beside the fire in the bar, reserved for the ghost; although he is rarely seen these days and only infrequently does the odd sound or curious incident remind the residents that the inn may be haunted.

Malpas, near Truro, Cornwall

There is a large, detached house here, about a century old, overlooking the Truro River, that has both a sinister history and a sinister reputation.

During World War II the property was requisitioned and used by the military as an ammunition store in case of invasion and accordingly the place was guarded day and night. Sometimes members of the Home Guard, including an uncle of Peter Barrett, a very reliable man and an electrician by trade – he was born in Malpas – took on the responsibility of looking after these premises. Footsteps that had no natural explanation were repeatedly heard by various people; they clearly came from the upper parts of the house, and so did the sound of doors opening and closing. All this at a time when the house was completely empty of human inhabitants inside and was securely guarded outside.

Time after time quiet and efficient investigation was carried out immediately the sounds were heard, but no one was ever discovered inside the house, no explanation was ever found for the sounds heard and the sounds invariably ceased when the house was entered.

Things became so bad that many of the young Home Guard volunteers would not go on duty at night-time. Various attempts were made

to placate the entity or entities causing the noises and when one particular door was found repeatedly opened after it had been carefully
closed, it was purposely left open – whereupon it would be closed!
And other doors left open that continually slammed shut by themselves were carefully closed, whereupon they opened by themselves!

Some years ago an informant told me that the house was in need of
renovation and after being in one family for many years it had recently been sold. I have often wondered whether the change of ownership
and any structural alterations and intensive renovation might have
affected the ghostly inhabitants.

A narrow lane leading towards a cottage that was once the village
public house used to be haunted by the ghost of a former inhabitant
who regularly walked down the lane during his lifetime. On one occasion the dead man's brother saw and heard the lifelike form, dead for
several years.

Membury, Devon

The old but well-preserved Quaker meeting-house has long been said
to harbour the quiet ghosts of some of the Puritan members of the
religious sect that once taught here, by example, peace and simplicity.
There is no mistaking these Quaker ghosts for their dress and general
appearance are distinctive and most of the local people will admit that
they are sometimes seen.

Another ghost appearance also concerns the good Quakers. Near
the part of the village known as Furley there is a long-disused Quaker
burial ground; a corner of a field, unconsecrated ground as was their
custom, and the name they called it was Calvary.

Some 30 years ago, a brother and sister were walking along the lane
away from Furley one bright summer day when they met two women
coming towards them; two women who looked, they thought, like
nuns, and they were carrying a large but plain and simply construct-
ed wooden cross.

Somewhat puzzled as to what the nuns were doing with their
strange burden, the brother and sister stopped after they had passed
and watched the two figures disappear round a bend in the road. As
they stood watching, a man they knew came round the corner towards

them. When they asked him what he thought the two nuns were doing, their friend looked puzzled and asked what they were talking about. He had seen no nuns; in fact the lane had been totally deserted apart from the brother and sister whom he had seen ahead of him before he reached the corner.

The youngsters were quite certain about what they had seen; they had both witnessed the same thing at the same time in bright daylight and they related their experience to a villager who they knew was interested in local history. He listened to what they had to say and then said he thought they must have seen two ghosts. Thinking back, the brother and sister could not recall having heard any sound as the two figures passed them and the nuns had certainly taken no notice of them – almost as though they were invisible.

The old villager suggested the figures they had seen were not nuns at all but two Quakers on their way to Calvary. The old Quaker burial ground at Furley was used as a burial pit for victims of the plague at Axminster and elsewhere, and Quakers were the only sect brave enough to bury those who died from the plague. When they were going to collect bodies and take them for burial the Quakers would carry a large wooden cross so that other people would know what they were doing and keep away.

Newton Abbot, Devon

Nearby Forde (or Ford) House, dating from 1610, is a graceful and elegant property where heavy tramping footsteps, like those of a heavily-booted man, have been repeatedly reported; phantom footsteps, that may be those of a king, passing up and down the corridors and rooms. It is said that William of Orange stayed at Forde House after his landing at Brixham in 1689, spending his first worried night on English soil, full of anguish and suffering great anxiety of mind that night, not knowing whether his expedition would succeed or fail.

At the beginning of a perilous venture, his contrasting hopes and fears may well have caused him to tramp restlessly up and down the house, exactly as the equally restless footsteps have tramped ever since. King William III never had any love for England, except as a treasure-chest and as an arsenal for his foreign wars. Once he was king he spent as little time as possible in England. Understandably, then, he was not a popular king and his unpleasant manners and ruthless nature did not help matters. Perhaps, if the phantom footsteps are his, there is an element of poetic justice in the fact that after death he is condemned to haunt the country from which he chose to absent himself as much as possible when he was alive.

Occasionally, on calm and still nights, but more frequently in stormy weather, it is said the footsteps long attributed to William III can be heard hurriedly passing up and down the corridors and through the empty rooms of this ancient house.

Ottery St Mary, Devon

Samuel Taylor Coleridge (1772-1834) was born in this ancient, famous and beautiful place, where his father was vicar and headmaster of the Grammar School. In fact there is much to interest the visitor, including Tudor Cadhay House with its perfect quadrangle and figure of Henry VIII with his three children, but we must make our way to the impressive church, a thirteenth-century building with a weathercock as old as the oldest stone in the whole edifice, which whistles in a strong wind.

Inside one of the finest churches in the county there is a minstrels' gallery, a season clock and a statue in the north aisle to Captain Coke, who died in 1632, supposedly murdered by his own brother to obtain an inheritance.

Be that as it may, at midnight on certain nights of the year, the spectacular coloured statue is said to come to life, step down from the monument and run round the church. It is a legendary story whose origin is lost in the mists of time. There are theories which suggest that some ghostly manifestations, after a long period, run down almost like a battery, and although the visual aspects disappear, the aural attributes remain. Interestingly enough there have been a number of reported incidents of unexplained running footsteps at night inside this lofty church.

Penryn, Cornwall

On a certain night each year, the bell of St Gluvias' Church has long been said to ring a melancholy knell when it is not possible for any human being to be responsible. Certainly no bellringers are at the church at the unearthly hour when the ringing is heard, clear and distinct above the sound of any wind or rain; in fact most of the local bellringers have long been careful to ensure that they are nowhere in the vicinity on that particular night, for the villagers and others believe the ringing can be put down to the ghost of Captain Martin, master of the Penryn barque *J B Gray* which foundered, with all hands, off the Bay of Biscay in 1890.

The story was recounted by a retired Royal Navy Commander at a meeting of the Ghost Club Society some fifty years ago. Commander A P Robinson heard the true story from his father who had known all the people concerned and the Dr Blamey involved was the Robinson family physician.

During his lifetime, Cornishman Martin had been a regular and loyal member of St Gluvias' congregation, where he was also a bellringer. For years after he was drowned he would return, it was said, to the old church that he loved and toll the bell on the anniversary of his passing from this world to the next.

One year Dr Blamey, who lived at Kernwick House near Penryn, and a friend of his, George Truscott from Falmouth, decided to sit up in the old church on the night of the reputed haunting. They agreed to meet at the lych gate at midnight, enter the church, and sit in the captain's old pew until two o'clock in the morning. If nothing had happened by then they would abandon the vigil.

On the day in question Blamey was summoned to Truro for consultation on a serious medical operation. As it was an emergency, he drove to the conference but his return was delayed until very late in the evening. However, he managed to get to Penryn before midnight and drove straight to the church. There he waited by the lych gate for his friend and within moments Truscott had joined him.

They walked quietly up the pathway together and entered the church by the transept door. Both men found themselves strangely disinclined to talk, but made their way directly to the captain's pew where Blamey occupied the actual seat while his friend sat near him.

After half an hour of silent vigil they both heard the muffled and spasmodic sound of a bell tolling, rising and falling with the howl of the wind which had risen since they had entered the church. The doctor nudged his companion but Truscott made no response and sat apart, apparently wrapped in thought. By one-thirty nothing further had occurred and both men silently left the church and went their separate ways home.

Dr Blamey slept on the couch in his surgery to avoid disturbing his wife and next morning, at breakfast, she greeted him with some surprising news.

'After you left for Truro yesterday,' she said, 'I received a telegram from Mrs Truscott at Falmouth. About three o'clock yesterday afternoon George Truscott died suddenly, of heart failure.'

Did a dead man keep an appointment with his friend for a ghost hunt? It is interesting that the 'ghost' of George Truscott did not, apparently, speak throughout the whole episode.

Penryn also has the reputation of being haunted by a ghostly coach drawn by headless horses, which have been reported to have been seen on many occasions but always just before Christmas.

Christina Hole, the respected folklorist and prominent member of the Folklore Society, once told me that she thought there was scarcely an old road in all England along which a spectral coach had not reportedly trundled at some time or another; sometimes, it was said, to fetch away the dying, sometimes as a conveyance for the already dead. It is always black and so are the driver and the horses; often both are headless. It appears suddenly, moves very fast and usually without noise. Often it is regarded as ominous and as a death-omen for those who encounter it.

Powderham, Devon

The castle here was for generations the home of the Courtenays, Earls of Devon, who obtained their name from a 'William wi' the short nose' (*court nez*) who fought against the Saracens and was accounted a saint. The church has long been reputedly haunted by a shrouded figure that has been seen, sometimes in the road outside, sometimes in the vicinity of the church gate and sometimes in the churchyard.

There are numerous reports of such a figure being seen near the church and some years ago a business man driving past saw a 'shrouded figure' in the roadway; a figure that disappeared as he approached. The same man reported seeing the same figure passing through the church gate and into the churchyard.

Another account tells of three people watching a grey shrouded figure which seemed to disappear in the churchyard; two weeks later the same three witnesses asserted they saw the same figure again and it disappeared in the same place as before.

A former rector was walking through the churchyard with a friend when they both saw two figures ahead of them. The rector's friend thought at first it was his wife and daughter, but as they drew nearer both figures suddenly disappeared. The rector, in relating the experience, always mentioned that, oddly enough, three weeks after seeing the mysterious forms, this friend's daughter died very suddenly and was buried in Powderham churchyard.

Sticklepath, Okehampton, Devon

A correspondent, living in a fairly large house here, tells me that when she and her family moved in two years previously, they were told that the 200-year-old property was haunted by a female ghost.

In 1940 the family then living in the house, which has changed hands many times, reported seeing the ghost which was described by the mother as 'a sort of white outline'. The same lady claimed her slippers and dressing gown were moved time and time again from one side of the room to the other.

Soon after the present occupants moved in, they were troubled by doors closing by themselves. At first they thought it must be due to the wind, but when the same thing happened to the same door on still and windless evenings they had to think again. They were also aware that occasionally their pet dogs would become alert and stare at the door, seeming to look through it and to be waiting for someone to appear. They would stay in this alert position, not moving a hair for a long time, just watching and waiting, and then eventually they would become more relaxed and go back to sleep.

One evening, only my correspondent's mother was in the house. She was reading and the dogs were in the garden. It was a still and quiet night, and suddenly she became aware of footsteps walking across the bedroom overhead – the same bedroom where a previous occupant had experienced movement of objects. The footsteps were loud and distinct, exactly as might be made by a human being, but she knew she was the only human being in the house. She was not unduly frightened however and after a while the footsteps ceased.

Not long afterwards, my correspondent was in the garage and her father and mother were in the house together with her brother when all of a sudden everyone inside heard a really loud crashing sound, almost as though the roof had fallen in. My informant's father hurriedly made his way to the attic but not only was the roof firm and undamaged, nothing had fallen, nothing had been moved and there was no possible explanation for the alarming sound. He came down from the loft and a few moments later there was another loud crashing sound!

Thereafter the family thought that perhaps the ghost was upset and angry because of many changes in the house, but after these two loud and quite inexplicable crashing sounds nothing further untoward happened.

Stogumber, Somerset

There is a lane, leading to a cottage, about a mile-and-a-half from Stogumber that seems to be haunted by a pleasant but ghostly odour.

A few years ago a correspondent, a very practical person who regards herself as far from psychic and says this is, in fact, the first and only experience of anything approaching psychic activity she has encountered, wrote to me about this scent.

While waiting for their house to be built at Sampford Brett, my correspondent and her husband rented a cottage near Stogumber. She frequently used to walk the pleasant lane leading to the village when she needed stamps, groceries and so on.

One day, in mid-December, a grey but perfectly still day, she was returning home with a basket of groceries, thinking of nothing except the food she and her husband would be having for supper that night, and the fact that it would soon be Christmas and their daughter would be arriving from abroad – calling for a rather special effort that year! So, pleasantly occupied with such thoughts as whether to have a goose or a turkey, she reached the foot of a small rise about half-a-mile from the cottage, at the top of which there was a small lane leading to an isolated farm – but this was out of sight.

Suddenly, my informant tells me, she became aware of a delightful smell; it reminded her of an expensive scent or cosmetics, such as one used to notice in the foyer of a London theatre in the days when people dressed for such an occasion. It was quite definitely an artificial scent, as of some kind of cosmetic; most certainly not any flower or plant – in fact in mid-December there simply was nothing to account for it.

My correspondent quietly put down her basket and walked over to the other side of the lane, to see whether the delightful odour persisted. It did, and it extended for a distance of a few feet either way. She was enjoying the sensation, and wondering where on earth it could have originated, when she heard the loud tread of what she took to be a man approaching the bend at the top of the little hill and coming towards her.

Thinking how stupid she would look, wandering about in the middle of the lane, ostensibly doing nothing, she hurriedly picked up her basket and went to meet whoever was approaching – and there was nobody! She thought it must have been someone from the farm who had disappeared down the track but she was wrong. Apart from the farm there were no houses at all along the whole one-and-a-half miles, nor, as far as she knew, had there ever been.

On later occasions, my correspondent tells me, she has often tried to recapture this lovely perfume, going to the same place at the same time, at the same season and in the same climate, but she has never succeeded in having this peculiar sensory experience again.

Swell, Fivehead, near Taunton

Some years ago now I heard that Commander John R Hoover had seen a ghostly female form at the Old Rectory, had heard inexplicable footsteps and had experienced other sounds and incidents for which he was at a complete loss to find a rational explanation. In 1986 he was good enough to acquaint me with some of his experiences. He told me he bought the house originally in 1959, and after spending a few years at sea he returned to live there permanently in 1964. The 'visitations' occurred infrequently and intermittently, sometimes with a lapse of two years, while in other years, for no known reason, they happened several times.

Commander John Hoover seemed to be the only member of his family to experience the presence and he was always alone in the house when it occurred, with the exception of the family cats and dog. The event always took place during the winter months, always in the evening, and usually as the Commander sat in the small study which, a hundred years ago, would have served as the kitchen of the house.

Commander Hoover told me that 'it' used to begin when he seemed to hear soft footsteps in the upstairs hall and then on the stairs, the foot of which is just outside the study door. This was followed by a gentle, but not cold, rush of air as though the study door had just been opened. The animals, if asleep, awakened at this stage and peered about the room, interested, as though a member of the family had just come in; but they were not agitated or distressed, and soon they settled down again.

If the Commander was sitting on the settee, there was a strange feeling of movement on the cushion next to him as though someone had just sat down and this was often accompanied by the 'soft sigh, as of a woman'. After an hour or so the reverse took place. Commander Hoover told me that he was always fully aware of the presence and felt nothing sinister in any of it, nor did he feel in the least frightened. Since the animals were not alarmed, he felt that the presence must be that of a 'friendly, saddened soul looking for help or company'. The footsteps, the sighs and the soft pressure on the cushion of the settee, Commander Hoover explained, were definitely those of a woman.

He had been told that during the nineteenth century a young kitchen maid lived in the nearby manor house, the fifteenth-century Swell Court, and used to cross the fields next to the Old Rectory to visit her young gentleman friend who lived at Fivehead, a mile away. He worked and lived at a manor house there called Cathanger, another house of great age. The story goes that the young man jilted his kitchen maid and she is said to have taken her own life; she was very friendly with the kitchen maid who then lived at The Rectory and the love-lorn girl often visited her friend – they used to meet in the room that is now the study.

Commander Hoover told me he was always convinced there was a presence in the house and he did not mind the smiles and scepticism of his friends. However, on two occasions in recent years he has met strangers who knew of the house and past owners – there have only been three others – and after hearing the place described, have referred to it as 'the haunted house'. Evidently previous owners have spoken about a presence in the house but since they are all now dead there is no way of verifying this.

Commander Hoover went on to say that in view of all this it is strange that other members of his family never experienced the phenomenon, but he liked his ghost and looked forward to her visits – he had even tried to converse with her but, he told me, 'as you may appreciate, we do not appear to be on the same communications frequency'.

Treslothan, Cornwall

The former vicarage – it has since been sold – was long reputed to be haunted. A former vicar there for seven years, the Reverend Peter Lafevre Eustice, tells me that the ghost was thought to be a mid-Victorian lady by the name of Tryphena Pendarves.

I first heard of the case from Air Commodore R Carter Jonas who in turn heard something of the story from Squadron Leader Flann. He reported the fact that a woman, wearing what might be medieval dress, had been seen in the vicarage study. Mr Peter Eustice tells me that Tryphena Pendarves had been a dominant, matriarchal figure. After her death her ghost was said to have been seen, sometimes somewhat mysteriously, in the vicarage study and, at other times, seemingly 'issuing from the family tomb adjacent to the church and walking the paths of her estate'.

The vicarage dates from 1840, I am told, 'although in the reens nearby are sited the archaeological remains of the ancient pilgrimage chapel of St Eia, excavated by Professor Charles Thomas and written up in his book, *Christian Antiquities of Camborne*.'

Mr Peter Eustice goes on to say that 'several people down the years have claimed to see Tryphena, and the late Father Ramsden Whalley – a predecessor of my informant as Vicar of Treslothan – seems to have made much of it and it is likely that Mr Flann heard it from him'. Mr Flann was the churchwarden of a neighbouring parish in those days.

Mr Eustice tells me however, 'Tryphena was not a disturbing influence and the churchyard was always a most peaceful spot.'

Wadebridge, Cornwall

In 1985 my wife and I visited a 250-year-old house in a village near Wadebridge where a series of strange happenings had taken place.

The family had moved into the house some ten months earlier and that first evening they understandably went to bed completely exhausted. Nevertheless both husband and wife were awakened in the middle of the night by odd sounds, which seemed to originate just outside their bedroom door; odd snuffling, rustling, uneven sounds. After a while the noises stopped and they went back to sleep, telling themselves that a door must have been left open and the dog had made its way upstairs. But in the morning the dog was asleep where it had been left and every door was firmly closed. However they learned that their daughter had been awakened during the night by what sounded like someone walking up and down outside and past her bedroom door.

A week later, five large ornamental spoons that hung on special hooks in the kitchen were found to have been removed from the wall and laid in a row below the hooks. No one in the house had touched the spoons. The same evening the family went into the sitting room to have coffee after their meal and they found all the ornaments that had been arranged around the fireplace had been moved to other places about the room; this, like the movement of the spoons, was equally inexplicable.

A few nights later some friends came for an evening meal and a sort of impromptu seance was held, but it was soon abandoned when a cigarette lighter 'blew up' and the eyes of two of the 'sitters' began to water uncontrollably and inexplicably.

Now, very sensibly, the occupants began to keep a diary of events. They noted that occurrences tended to take place with some degree of regularity; often things would happen on a Tuesday, to be followed by a period of inactivity until the Saturday, then peace again until the following Tuesday, and so on. Over the next few weeks objects were repeatedly moved, particularly in one bedroom and on the stairs; the objects around the fireplace in the sitting room were moved again and sometimes members of the household independently said they had the impression of 'something horrible' in the dining room.

One evening, every object in a room was examined and its position recorded; shortly afterwards some of the objects had been moved. It was noticed that objects made of wood were rarely moved whereas anything made of silver seemed to attract the attention of whatever was moving the articles. It was also noticed that practically everything that was moved was a personal object, either a present or a personal purchase; household items were usually left alone. The family also noticed that it was rare for the same object to be moved more than once.

One Saturday morning, both husband and wife were downstairs and alone in the house when they heard the sounds of someone or something walking about in the upstairs corridor; back and forth the sounds seemed to go, just like someone walking the length of the corridor and then returning and beginning again. Quickly and quietly they both made their way upstairs; the sounds became softer and then ceased and in one bedroom a number of objects had been moved.

Sometimes, in the presence of a friend who was in the police force, the resident dog would become transfixed and stare up at a corner of the room near a door; once a vase of dried flowers moved about twelve inches upwards; the next day two ornamental jar lids were moved. On another occasion a big modern picture hanging in the bathroom 'jumped' off the wall and was found wedged between two taps. It is an exceptionally large picture and it is difficult to imagine how it could have moved from its hooks and finished up where it did.

A copper picture 'moved itself' upstairs and was found in the hollow between two beams six feet from the floor. A visitor felt her hair rise on the back of her neck for no apparent reason; all she knew was that she felt terrified. Her husband went to the bathroom and returned to say he had had a very puzzling experience. He thought he had heard a cleaner being used on the landing and, thinking this unlikely, he had quietly opened the bathroom door. The sound had ceased instantly.

The following Tuesday many objects were moved in the dining room; cushions were found pushed about as though someone had been sitting in all the chairs. Some of the cushions and some of the articles were discovered outside the dining room.

Other puzzling and very frightening incidents included one occasion when the lady of the house felt somehow imprisoned in her own kitchen. She was too frightened to leave it all day; what she was frightened of she did not know. Once, on entering the dining room on a cool autumn day, it was discovered that the temperature in the room was extremely warm, unnaturally and unbearably warm. Another time, on a still and quiet day, one of the occupants suddenly broke out in goose pimples and holding up her arms she felt a soft wind move through the room in a circular, sudden and very frightening manner. On another occasion eight people in the house stood stock still and a wind wound its way in and out of them, unmistakable and quite inexplicable; all the doors and windows at the time were closed, yet everyone felt freezing cold as long as the wind was in the room.

Some friends suggested holding a seance at the house and when this was done a story unfolded that could have explained some of the peculiar happenings. An entity calling 'herself' Kay said she had murdered her son, Peter, in the house by poisoning him; afterwards she had burned the body and buried the remaining fragments under the floor of the dining room. She maintained that the present occupant's husband reminded her of past days and she wanted the present lady of the house out of the property. The 'spirit' Kay stubbornly refused to

leave the house herself but eventually accepted that the present occu-
piers had a right to live in peace.

When they first moved in, the present occupants thought about
taking up the floor of the dining room and re-laying it with new
wood, but now they did not feel they dare interfere with the flooring
– they were afraid they might find the remains of a body there.

The wife became more and more frightened by the events and the
atmosphere in the house. She felt very strongly that whatever was in
her home did not want her to stay and would do almost anything to
get her out for good. In her distress she approached the church but
they only suggested she contact a local bishop.

That evening the disturbances were far worse than they had ever
been. After their meal our informant said she was so scared that she
could not leave the dining room to make the coffee, so her husband
went out to make it. A moment later he returned, his eyes staring and
his face flushed… In the kitchen he had been very aware that some
presence was there too.

Back in the dining room he sat down on the settee and then suddenly fell back, his mouth opening wider and wider and he was obviously not in control of himself. His wife grabbed hold of him, only to
find him rigid and unaware of her. She was terrified but eventually
pulled him forward and he gradually became aware of his surroundings again – but he had no recollection of the past moments and could
not tell his wife why he had felt so frightened or what had happened
to him. He said that after entering the kitchen he had felt there was
something odd about the room but telling himself not to imagine
things he had gone towards the fridge. Suddenly he had felt very ill
and very cold; he knew his mouth was open but he could not close it;
he felt as though words were about to come out of his mouth but he
could not speak; then it had left him and he had made the coffee, but
when he had taken it into the dining room, it had all happened again
and he did not remember anything else. Looking back they had
noticed that things often started up after they talked about the flooring in the dining room.

They decided to move into the sitting room and they started to
move the coffee things there when both of them suddenly felt drained

of energy; almost as soon as they were aware of it, it was all over and they felt fine again. Then they felt something come towards them from the direction of the dining room; their dog showed every sign of being terrified and his mouth dropped open.

Husband and wife staggered back to the settee in the sitting room and they managed to find a couple of crucifixes and they waved them about. When they found that this seemed to help, they systematically went round the room and paid especial attention to the corners which they felt might harbour something unpleasant. They found they were less worried when their feet were on the ground. Back on the settee our informant's husband was in a terrible state and she felt that the only solution was for them all to get out of the house, but he would not hear of leaving. Gradually the atmosphere improved and after an almost sleepless night, with the lights on, crucifixes spread about the room and sudden breezes blowing in circles round their faces, at six o'clock in the morning the wife telephoned her mother and they all went to stay with her for a week.

While they were away they arranged for the whole house to be blessed by an archbishop. Thereafter they had no disturbances for two and a half months and then, in the middle of December, it all started up again.

There was quite a large family gathering at the house. As everyone was helping to decorate the place and prepare for the festive season, one after the other they complained of the feeling of being watched and followed; it was as if something invisible was behind each of them in turn in various parts of the house. They noticed too, whenever they were conscious of the strange 'something' near them, that they felt extremely cold. One night as they sat in front of a roaring open fire they were freezing cold. Then, from time to time for several weeks they experienced strange smells of gas and other inexplicable odours, particularly in the main bedroom where a heavy perfume like roses would suddenly surround them and then as suddenly disappear.

In the dining room at this period they all noticed, when there was no fire, a smell of burning; there was no smoke and nothing in the house that could have accounted for such a smell which in any case was localised and especially prevalent in one area of the dining room.

During the following January and February, three times in one week, the residents felt the breeze playing on their faces as they had done before the house was blessed. 'At times it was like icy fingers on the temple, squeezing.'

They were away from the house for a week; when they returned the atmosphere had completely changed and they had no further incidents. Once or twice they felt the awful atmosphere beginning to return but they willed themselves to be brave and ignore it and it seemed to go away. Occasionally at night the breezes would return and play in circular motions over their faces; then they would put their faces under the bedclothes and after a while the breeze disappeared.

One day the lady of the house had a friend in for lunch (to whom she had said nothing about any of the odd happenings) and as soon as she entered the dining room this friend started to shake violently. She said she was sensitive to atmosphere and asked whether they had experienced any strange happenings in the house; being conscious of psychic atmosphere, she occasionally saw and heard things that were not visible or audible to other people. She did not like many parts of the house, especially the dining room, and immediately pointed out most of the places where things had moved by themselves. She said there was an accusing atmosphere in the house.

When they went upstairs a sudden gust of wind blew out of nowhere and surrounded them and the visitor said, 'Can't you hear her laughing?' She had a clear picture of a tiny, youngish woman, dressed in brown and wearing an apron; she did not think she was an evil or unkind person but she wanted the present occupants out of the house.

This visitor also felt that there was something decidedly unpleasant about the fireplace and its surround, and this is where many odd things had happened. She thought it was possible that a spirit or ghost was somehow attached to the fireplace. She was also alarmed at something in the house that had come from old Bodmin Jail.

She said that one of two panelled rooms that join was more haunted than the other and this was correct; indeed as my wife and I walked about the house we felt a very odd atmosphere in some parts and a very different feeling in others. We both thought one part of the stairway distinctly odd and as we came down these stairs both of us felt a definite breeze on our faces. As we stopped and turned we saw some dried flowers in a vase moving as though in a breeze. On the landing, as we made our way up we saw what appeared to be a smoke haze but there was no smell and it cleared as mysteriously as it appeared.

In one bedroom, which we immediately said we liked the least of any room in the house, we were told that a friend who had been staying was reading a book one night when she saw the lamp move – and watched it move from one side of the bedside table to the other in front of her eyes!

As soon as we had entered the dining room both my wife and I had the impression 'I want to get out of here'. We didn't go immediately but after we had heard everything we could about the odd happenings at this, to all appearances, very pleasant house, and had toured it completely, we found that we were not sorry to leave.

West Quantoxhead, near Taunton, Somerset

Beverley Nichols lived for many years on Ham Common, only a few miles from us when we lived in turn at Richmond, Twickenham, and at Strawberry Hill. My library contains several of his volumes which he inscribed for me, and we spent many hours in his beautiful garden. He was no stranger to ghosts and one of the weirdest experiences he related to me happened to his friend, Peter, and took place at the rambling, pleasant old house, known as St Audrie's, which was Peter's home, and, Beverley assured me, 'it is the unadulterated truth'.

Peter had returned home from one of his visits to London to find the large house deserted except for his sister and the servants. On his second night at home on this occasion he found himself feeling unusually tired, and so, around ten o'clock in the evening, he went to his room which lay at the end of a long corridor – some distance from the main body of the house – and within half-an-hour he was fast asleep.

Some hours later, in the middle of the night, he found himself suddenly wide awake with the distinct feeling that his sleep had been disturbed by a noise of some kind. As he lay listening, he heard a noise, apparently emanating from the corridor outside his room; yet, who on earth could it be at this time of night, he asked himself.

He called out but there was no answer. He called again but still there was no reply. Puzzled but determined to discover who or what had awakened him, he slipped out of bed, put on a dressing gown and opened his bedroom door.

Facing him in the corridor stood an old woman carrying a candle; she was standing only a few yards from him and seemed to regard him without surprise or embarrassment, looking hard at him with calm and wide-open eyes. Peter looked equally hard at her. He had never seen her before and he asked her who she was and what she was doing. When he received no reply he took a step towards her and, as he did so, she promptly turned and began to walk away from him down the long corridor. For the first time he felt there might be something odd about the form which certainly looked solid and real enough. He noticed that although she turned quite suddenly and was walking away quite quickly, the flame of the candle she was carrying seemed to be constant and still and unaffected by her movements.

His curiosity mounting, he began to follow and as he did so she seemed to break into a run. Thinking she meant to elude him, Peter started running too and he chased her down the long corridor towards the main portion of the house, along a passage, up a little staircase, along another passage; faster and faster the figure in front of him seemed to run.

At the far end of the house, when he was only a few yards behind her, she turned into a narrow passage that he knew led to a room from which there was no other way out. As she disappeared inside there was the sound of a door slamming – and a second later Peter flung the door open. The room was empty, silent, deserted and the still atmosphere told him that no human being was present, other than himself.

Puzzled and bewildered by the strange experience, Peter stood there wondering what the explanation could be. There was no doubt that the only exit to the room was by the door through which she – and he – had just entered. Unless, of course, she had jumped out of the window. He went over and looked out at the dark night.

He knew there was a sheer drop of over 40 feet to the lawn below.

The window was locked and barred; it looked as though nobody had opened it for years.

Peter shrugged his shoulders and walked back to his room, more than a little disturbed by the event. Back in his room he glanced at his watch and saw that the time was two minutes to one. He got back into bed and was soon asleep.

Next morning the whole adventure he remembered so vividly seemed so fantastic that he decided to say nothing about it to anyone, although he noticed that his dressing gown was thrown across a chair and the soles of his feet were dirty where he had run along dusty corridors; at all events it had not been a dream. He went downstairs, talked normally and cheerfully with his sister, and said nothing about the disappearing woman.

As he rose from the breakfast table his sister suddenly said: 'Oh Peter, the clock on the mantelpiece has stopped and it's a terrible nuisance to wind. What is the right time?' Peter looked at the clock.

The hands stood at two minutes to one. He took out his own watch – that too had stopped at two minutes to one. 'I'm not sure,' Peter replied. 'I'll go outside and tell you.' But in the hall the same thing had happened. The grandfather clock, reliable and precise for many years, had also stopped – at two minutes to one.

And in fact all the clocks in all the other rooms of St Audrie's had also stopped that night – at two minutes to one. Even a clock over the staircase, which could only be reached by a ladder and for which Peter alone held the key, had also stopped at two minutes to one.

'That is all,' Beverley Nichols told me. 'There is no explanation, no sequel of any kind; it just happened and as far as I know it never happened again.'

St Audrie's became a school and the headmaster, Mr A J Tough, BA, told me he had been there for ten years and was 'not aware of any such manifestations'. He added, 'I suppose all old houses acquire legends about ghosts…' True enough, and yet I wonder…

Whitestone, Exeter

The old Rectory, now known as The Glebe House, has been rumoured to be haunted, according to the *Transactions of the Devonshire Association* '28th Report on Folklore', for at least 150 years. The old house ceased to be the Rectory in 1958.

Mr John West who lived at the house told me that the Whitestone Rectory records do not, to his recollection, refer in detail to ghostly happenings, 'although the neighbouring lane is the subject of legend and one of my sons had an "experience" some years ago, but apart from this I can only report that the atmosphere of the house is excellent and totally in keeping with the long line of good men and their families who have inhabited the Rectory'.

However, according to the aforementioned Report, the ghost is said to have been seen flying out of a window wearing the master's hat and wig on one occasion when an attempt was made to exorcise it!

Yealmpton, South Devon

One evening during the summer of 1985, I saw a report on Yealmpton, witnessed by the vicar and his wife. I immediately contacted the Reverend Dr A T P Byles and he has been good enough to let me have full details of the curious experience.

One Saturday afternoon, not long after her husband had become vicar of Yealmpton, Mrs Byles was busy arranging the altar flowers inside the church. Her husband was making his way along the path towards the door leading from the south side of the church, as he wished to speak to her.

Suddenly, in the middle of the path in front of him, he noticed a hole of irregular shape, about a yard in width. Thinking it must be the result of subsidence, he picked his way round the hole, which seemed to be very deep, and went into the church and told his wife what he had seen.

Having talked to her for a moment the vicar thought he would have another look at the rather dangerous hole in the path and, leaving his wife, he went outside. When he reached the hole he was somewhat surprised and not a little disturbed to find that the hole was very much larger. He hurriedly returned to his wife and asked her to come and see it.'

They both looked into the hole and the vicar suggested lowering himself into it but, not knowing its depth and how safe it might be, he decided against this course of action. He did throw a stone into the hole in an attempt to judge its depth, and they both noticed that the stone bumped against stonework, which they found they could see and which looked like a wall.

The vicar's main concern was to prevent any possibility of an accident to anyone using the path who would be unaware of the sudden hole, so he went away to find some planks to cover it until he could get some workmen to deal with the matter in a more permanent way. To ascertain the length of the planks he would require he measured the diameter of the hole and found it to be more than nine feet across.

In the village street he met Mr Knight, the local builder, and also the undertaker, and he told them both about the mysterious hole and asked them to come and see it so that he could judge how best to deal with it.

When they arrived there was no sign of the hole!

The path and grass verge were exactly as they had been before the hole had appeared. There was no sign of any disturbance to the earth or the grass or the path itself. Mr Knight, the vicar tells me, seemed less puzzled than might have been expected, hurriedly left and never mentioned the incident again. The Reverend Dr Byles, MA, PhD, wrote an account of the incident which was published in the *Transactions of the Devonshire Association*, Volume CVII, page 190.

Dr Byles told me: 'Yealmpton Vicarage, a Queen Anne house near the church, has its mysteries too. We used to hear footsteps on the stairs, as on bare boards, although the stairs were carpeted. There was also a room on the first floor which gave all who slept there nightmares and a sensation of an evil presence. This was felt by my son – then about sixteen – my brother and myself. In fact nobody completed a night's sleep in that room, though it showed no unusual features by day…'